The Ghosts of Brixham

Graham Wyley

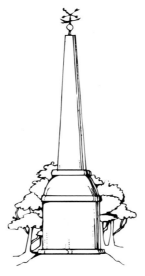

OBELISK PUBLICATIONS

We have over 170 Devon-based titles, for a current list please send an s.a.e. to the address given below or telephone (01392) 468556.

PLATE ACKNOWLEDGEMENTS
Jane Reynolds for cover drawings and pages 15 and 26;
Chips Barber supplied pictures on pages 17, 28, 29 and 30;
Graham Wyley for all other pictures.

First published in 1991, reprinted in 2000 by
Obelisk Publications, 2 Church Hill, Pinhoe, Exeter, Devon EX4 9ER
Designed by Chips and Sally Barber
Edited and Typeset by Sally Barber
Printed in Great Britain

Introduction

In the course of my seemingly never-ending investigations into ghostly goings-on or haunted happenings, I am frequently called upon to witness at first hand the sort of experience which would give most people nightmares! I have stayed in haunted farmhouses, castles, dungeons, hotels and private homes – and invariably I am locked in to prove that I have no fear of these often unwanted spectral intruders.

By the very nature of my work, I have been "on call" at any time to help anyone who may be concerned or in distress through a troublesome haunting. It has led me to visit many interesting places and to encounter some strange and bizarre happenings. Many television, radio and film personalities have called on my services and it has been my privilege and pleasure to help them.

But in this book it is not to the glamorous world of glittering lights and big star names we look, but to my home town of Brixham in Devon, full of down-to-earth, straight-talking "ordinary" folk. Brixham sits snugly in a deep depression between the high hills and seems as peaceful and untroubled as any settlement could be. However, some prolonged probing has revealed that close-knit Brixham, the Mother of the Deep Sea Fisheries, has more than its fair share of spooks – enough to fill a small book! Throughout the town's narrow streets, with their quaint old houses steeped in history, still reside some of its long-gone residents who seem rather reluctant to leave – but then who can blame them for wanting to stay in such a lovely old town?

The author relating a hair-raising experience to his good friend Burt Kwouk, versatile actor from Goldfinger *and the "Pink Panther" movies.*

The French Connection – Baker's Hill

Even in our wildest dreams we cannot begin to imagine the misery, degradation, squalor and poverty associated with the Brixham Workhouse at Baker's Hill in the early 1600s. Here, entire families, homeless children and isolated individuals were housed, fed and kept alive at the expense of the church and local community.

When the Poor Law was passed in 1601 it was decreed that each parish should have its own workhouse to care for these unfortunate, down-and-out people and it was deemed that the local residents would be compelled to pay rates towards the upkeep of this establishment. This arrangement was to be in existence for well over two hundred years.

During their stay, young children sat at benches on the cobbled stone floor in the dark and dismal area below ground, where all day long they would pick oakum – tarred ropes used for caulking the seams of ships. Sometimes their only companion would be a trouble-maker or mentally deranged individual, chained and shackled with a leg iron to the wall close by.

It was around this time that the occasional French sailor would be captured and imprisoned under the same roof as the workhouse families – that was until it was considered safe for him to be put out in the fields to work on a surrounding farm under close supervision.

Many of these sailors would never see their native land again, for they would die, sometimes tragically, before being released. It would seem that one of these seafaring men has decided to retain his "presence" in the building to this very day.

When the workhouse finally closed in 1834 it lay abandoned for many years until the turn of the century, when it became a school. Directly after the end of the Second World War, the Royal British Legion took it over for their headquarters. It was then that the "happenings" seemed to start – and have continued ever since …

During the 1980s Bruce, who was then the cleaner at the "Legion", used to start work at around 5.30 in the morning. He recalls that there was one dark winter's morning that he will never forget for the rest of his life …

It all started when he went downstairs to unlock the door to the billiard room, for when he pushed it open and put on the light, there, by the old fireplace at the end of the snooker table, was seated a tall grey-haired sailor dressed in an old-fashioned blue smock.

Bruce's first impulse was to ask the visitor whether "He had been locked in all night?" Whereupon the old gent stood up, the faint hint of a smile breaking across his weather-beaten face as he faded into the fireplace, and was gone, leaving Bruce standing there spellbound.

It was not until this incident was related that other members agreed that they too had often experienced the feeling of a cold unnatural atmosphere, as if someone was watching them, when down in this area.

Not content with just making his presence felt, the ghost, who by now was being regularly referred to as "François", concentrated his attentions on becoming mischievous and aggravating, by performing harmless pranks to authenticate his existence.

Peg Tribble found that the electricity supply was constantly being tampered with by our "friend", who waited until the vacuum cleaner was switched on and working before stopping the motor time and again.

During the Christmas period of 1988, Peg and Sheila were tidying up after midnight in the skittle alley, which is next to the billiard room. As usual the vacuum was playing up, so Peg announced firmly to François: "Come on now, we're tired; we don't mind you mucking about, but we've had enough!"

At that very moment everything started working again properly. It would seem that every time "he" decided to stage this strange exhibition, he had to be rebuked severely before normal service was resumed.

The members of the Brixham Royal British Legion accepted François with friendliness and tolerance and were of the general opinion that he was as entitled to occupy the building as they were.

The Early Morning Couple – Breakwater Beach

Every morning for over thirty years, whatever the weather, Grace would make the short journey down to Breakwater Beach, from her home close by, and have her customary swim before breakfast. Her arrival at the water's edge was as punctual as clockwork, for each day at 5.45 a.m. her solitary figure would be seen entering the water.

Six a.m. would find her enjoying a hot cup of tea from a flask as she sat and admired the peaceful, tranquil view towards Berry Head, before embarking on the journey home.

Then, in early June 1972, whilst taking in the picturesque surroundings, her attention was mysteriously drawn to the magnificent Woolborough House, situated directly above the beach. By the bushes on the driveway slope, she saw the stationary figures of a man and woman; he was dressed in a drab, grey-coloured suit and wearing an old-fashioned hat, whereas she had on a dark top, a shawl around her shoulders and a large black bonnet on her head, reminiscent of the Victorian era. Grace stared avidly at the two figures for several minutes until, to her utter amazement, without any warning, they both disappeared, right in front of her eyes. Although intrigued by what she assumed to be some sort of optical illusion, she was unable to offer any plausible explanation for the strange sighting.

The very next morning when Grace arrived on the beach, she made a point of curiously glancing up at the driveway and, as she had expected, it was completely deserted ... yet at precisely 6 a.m. the two figures again appeared, standing motionless, looking down at her!

On the third day, she rushed from the sea, sat down and waited in anticipation. As the chimes of All Saints Church rang out at six o'clock, the two figures again materialised in exactly the same spot and were visible for several minutes before weirdly vanishing into thin air.

Research has established that Woolborough House was built for a Mr Charles Hellier, a rich and successful merchant and ship owner. It was constructed from material obtained from the adjacent quarry and completed in 1912. At the beginning of June in that year, work started on the steep driveway. Early one morning, the driver of the steam roller had just climbed aboard his vehicle when he suddenly discovered that the brakes had failed; it careered down the slope and across the road, smashed through the wall and ended up on Breakwater Beach below.

The brave driver remained with his machine all through this harrowing ordeal, but sadly lost his life in the effort. The strange connection between this tragic accident and the sightings made by Grace was that it had been exactly sixty years before, almost to the day, that the driver had met his death. One wonders whether this poor man had returned in spirit, with his wife, to the exact spot where he had climbed aboard that ill-fated steam roller on the day he lost his life, all those years ago.

The Ghosts of Brixham

Alcohol is not the only Spirit – Main Street

In 1984 Sue and her husband began working as managers at an off-licence in one of the main streets of Brixham, but little did they know that the spirits on the premises were not just those of the bottled variety, for inexplicable "happenings" were soon to be encountered!

At times Sue found it necessary to enter the unoccupied rooms at the top of the building, and this was where she would experience a strange, unnaturally cold atmosphere prevailing. And as if this wasn't enough, she felt also that she was being watched by some invisible presence.

As the remainder of the staff were totally unaware of what was happening, it was treated as a joke, so much so that in a light-humoured attitude they christened Sue's ghost "Charlie", yet Sue's husband, who was a total sceptic on matters of the supernatural, dismissed the entire incident as an over-active imagination.

He was to change his opinion, however, some two years later, when at around 9 p.m. one dark evening, he too went up to the unoccupied rooms and suddenly felt the uncanny cold atmosphere surrounding him, and became aware of a hand resting on his shoulder – yet he could not see any other human being in the room with him!

Eighteen months later a team of stock-takers visited the off-licence, and during the evening one of them, totally unaware of the reputed hauntings, decided to explore the rooms at the top of the building. He went alone, but when he returned only a short while later he was trembling and his face was white with fear, for he too had experienced the same indisputable presence alone with him in that upstairs room.

From that very day on, no further strange occurrences took place, as if Charlie had taken a distinct liking to the stock-taker and decided to accompany him on his travels! We wish them both bon voyage …

Please, Don't Leave Me – New Road

A shop and adjoining house in New Road are no strangers to ghosts, for here, some years ago, the property was found to be haunted by a calm, reassuring apparition who wandered aimlessly throughout the property at will. The family accepted the presence without any fear or trepidation until, one day, it was joined by a dark, evil force which was determined to cause unrest, havoc and disruption amongst the household …

These activities became so disturbing that the local priest was summoned; he blessed the house and, to all intents and purposes, the hauntings ceased and peace and tranquillity were restored.

Eventually Gerald and Anna considered moving and discussed the matter at great length. It was not until they began to make positive plans, however, and also removed a cupboard under the stairs at the rear of the property, that a strange phenomenon manifested itself – the presence, at certain times of day, of an obnoxious smell. Experts were called in to examine the drains and pipework in this immediate area to try to ascertain what was causing the trouble, but after considerable investigation nothing untoward was discovered.

It was noticed that when estate agents visited, in order to obtain details, the smell would become most prolific and would only subside and finally disappear immediately after they had left, as if some sort of bizarre demonstration was being staged solely in their honour! When I visited the property at the request of the owners, it soon became apparent that the original calm, reassuring apparition was still very much in residence, although it had not been seen or heard since the priest's visit, for I became aware of its very existence, close by the back door.

Clearly the Earth-bound spirit had been reluctant to vacate the premises and had been quite content to remain dormant, for it had developed an association and acceptance with this family over the years. Now the family were considering moving, which was too much for the ghost to accept; in an effort to dissuade potential buyers, the "entity" was mysteriously creating the hideous odour, hoping that the property would not be sold!

As the situation was unacceptable, I advised them that the very next time the revolting smell appeared, they were to be firm and explain to the presence that due to ill health they were compelled to move. Although they would be sorry to leave, if the presence so desired they would be quite happy for "it" to accompany them to their new residence.

From that very day on, the disturbing, obnoxious smell was replaced by the mysterious scent of beautiful, strongly perfumed flowers, as if the situation had been resolved and accepted by the presence and this was its way of showing that it understood!

Reflecting Image – Church Hill West

When Joan commenced employment at the Smugglers Haunt Hotel, in March 1963, there were no guests checked in at the time. But she was soon to find out that the hotel had permanent visitors ...

Her very first incident was when she heard an unusual noise in the upstairs lounge and, upon investigation, found that the television set was on. Undaunted, she turned it off and removed the plug. Just ten minutes later she heard the identical sound and, to her utter amazement, upon entering the lounge, found the television plugged in and working!

A regular guest at the hotel described how, every night during his stay, he would switch on the light, only to find it turned itself off and, when he locked his room, the door would become unlocked for no logical reason. These incidents intensified at night – during the hours of darkness some invisible force would disturb his slumbers by pulling off the bedclothes.

Legend has it that in the early 1900s a young woman fell to her death, under mysterious circumstances, from the window of this very bedroom when it was a smuggler's cottage and, as a result, the strange happenings have been attributed to the ghost of this poor unfortunate lady. Over the years she has been affectionately referred to as "Aggie", even by those who have not had the pleasure of her presence.

The plate glass mirror on the far wall of the restaurant is where our next apparition makes "his" appearance. Both Joan and a previous chef have seen his reflection on several occasions, the last being in December 1988. He is described as of medium height, in his early forties, with long dark hair, on which is perched an old cloth cap. He is dressed in a grey, full-length raincoat, which extends right down to his ankles. Each time that his

reflection is observed he is always at the same table, where he is seen sometimes sitting, other times standing.

The kitchen area also seems to be blessed with its fair share of inexplicable experiences, for in here, not that long ago, a box containing surplus dishes raised itself from the shelf and, with uncanny precision, floated gently through the air and landed on the floor. A hand of bananas has also been observed in mid-air; gas taps turned on and off at will; and a series of prepared dessert dishes were seen to slide off the top of the freezer and slowly, one by one, fall to the floor!

On the night that I investigated the happenings, two strange incidents occurred. I was standing in the kitchen when, for no apparent reason, my holdall containing camera and recording tapes was indisputably propelled across the room. Even more strange was the photograph that I took in the "haunted" bedroom, for on the original print my own reflection could be seen in the mirror yet, when we looked at the same print nearly twenty months later, *I* had disappeared and my image had been replaced by the "ghost" of a young *lady*!

The Captain Remains? – Pring's Court

As I travel around this picturesque fishing town, meeting and talking with people, I am amazed at the sheer volume of ghosts, spirits or apparitions seen or experienced in this relatively small community. Perhaps, as its historical roots stem back so far, it has captured and retained more than its normal share of the supernatural.

The story I am about to relate falls into this category. In the 1830s Daniel Pring and his wife Elizabeth were blessed with a son, who was christened John Wheaton Pring.

The lad grew up to be a prosperous mariner and sea captain, to the extent that in 1870 the first of his ships, the *Jane Richardson*, a 269-tonne barque, was built. The following year he extended his nautical prowess and added the 242-tonne brigantine, *Ferdinande* to his accomplishments and, finally, in 1875 he had a purpose-built barque constructed. She was a 263-tonne vessel named *Annie*.

Captain Pring became a well-known figure in the town who commanded respect and admiration from his crews and fellow skippers. He resided at No 3, Pomeroy's Court, where he kept his safe in the upstairs rear bedroom, his meat store in a room off the front hall, and the pay office for his men directly outside the front door. All these facilities are still at the cottage to this day.

This man of substance must have made his mark on society for, at the turn of this century, the court which had been known as Pomeroy's for so many years was renamed Pring's Court.

The cottages in this small court, together with those directly behind, are said to have given safe haven to many a Brixham smuggler, and his illicitly acquired contraband, over the years since they were built in 1783.

Mr and Mrs Jack Meyer moved into No 3 in 1929, yet it was over fifty years, in 1983 in fact, before the first ghost appeared.

Jack got out of bed at around 2.00 a.m., destined for the toilet. He opened the bedroom door and stepped out onto the landing, only to be confronted by the sight of a shadowy male form leaning against the wall. Before he had time to gather his thoughts, Jack had walked right through this mysterious spook and on to the end of the landing.

Although he returned quickly to the spot, there was now no trace or evidence of the "visitor". He did explain to me that at the time he had experienced an extremely cold sensation, which he likened to "walking through a block of ice".

The next encounter, which was to manifest in a slightly different form, took place on 31 October of the same year when Jack Meyer was on his own. He recalls the event vividly.

He had been out working on that particular morning and upon arrival home found the cottage empty so, settling down in his favourite armchair in front of the fire in the parlour, which had been the old kitchen area many years before, he decided to take a nap.

As he was dozing off, he was awakened abruptly by the sound of voices in the same room and, as he explained in his own Devonshire dialect: "From one side of the room a woman's voice was yammering on about summit in a persistent manner, while her male companion simply replied 'oyes, oyes' complaisantly from the far corner; when I tried to make out who they were, the voices stopped."

Since that day everything has returned to normal, but who can say categorically that the "spirit" of – perhaps – Captain Pring, or even one of those dastardly smugglers, will not return to the cottage again without warning?

The Sweet-Toothed Spook – Drew Street

It was quite by accident that I uncovered the next story, for I had passed this property many times and had noted with curiosity the unusually shaped timber with carved letters which constituted part of the car port at the end of the building. So one day I took a closer look and discovered that it was one of the main timbers from an old fishing smack, showing her registration number and tonnage. Anxious to photograph this beam, I knocked at the door for permission.

This old dwelling is now separated into two homes; I was drawn towards the door of the main part of the building, and there met a lady known as "Dot" who had lived there for over forty years.

As I went through the front door it was like entering into a time warp, for very little had been altered in the three hundred years since this large property was constructed, even to the extent that the "Priest's Hole" (a secret hiding place in the time of persecution or repression) was still evident.

My attention was drawn to an inscription on the far wall which read: "This five foot thick wall is the end of the original house built in 1610 by A. Flavel, one of the original Pilgrim Fathers, who organised, yet did not sail on, the *Mayflower*. In 1720 the rear end of these premises were added to become the Lord Nelson Inn."

I have subsequently ascertained that this inn traded under the Torbay Brewery until its closure in 1880.

When Dot and her husband acquired this property in 1945, accommodation was almost impossible to find, yet this house had been empty for some considerable time, which they later found out was due to its unsavoury reputation. They were told that over a hundred years ago the house was steeped in illness of one kind or another, to the extent that on numerous occasions coffins were seen leaving the house in the direction of St Mary's Churchyard.

On this story, documentation later proved that the house had been used by the local smugglers as a storage centre for illicit contraband, and that each coffin that emerged had contained "spirits" of a liquid consistency en route to the churchyard before being sold.

During the Second World War, the father of a family who were residing in this house committed incest with his young daughter and was subsequently gaoled for the offence. The remainder of the family were taken into care by the Salvation Army. This incident appalled the neighbourhood so much that even the house was considered "unclean" and stood empty until 1945.

It had always been noticed that a decidedly chilly atmosphere was constant in the sitting room downstairs and that no form of additional heating could compensate for the temperature drop caused by this inexplicable phenomenon.

The regular disappearance of items of clothing had also added to the mystery surrounding this dwelling; everyday articles seemed to vanish for no apparent reason, only to reappear several days later in some obvious location entirely different to where they were placed originally.

One slightly more light-humoured, yet still incomprehensible, encounter took place about five years before our conversation, when Dot was on her own. She wanted to ice a cake she had made, yet search as she might, the icing set was not to be found so, undaunted, she located several pieces of stiff paper in an endeavour to produce her own conical funnels for the purpose of icing.

After laying the paper on the kitchen table, she went straight into the sitting room to get the scissors. On her return, to her total amazement, there were four already-constructed, perfectly made, cones on the table – which she said could only have been done by an unknown presence.

Over the years Dot came to terms with her invisible visitor and accepted him as part of the household, even to the extent that she nicknamed him "Charlie" and referred to him as being a very friendly and happy ghost whenever he was around.

The Conscientious Nanny – Burton Street

In Higher Brixham, which is the oldest part of the town, four similar late Georgian manor houses with identical windows were constructed in the early 1800s: these were Eveleigh, The Lodge, Aylmer and Burton Villa. It is in the last property that past happenings seemed to have been retained forever in the thick stone walls.

In order to offer some plausible explanation for this phenomenon, it was necessary to research its very existence, right back to the original construction in 1825, when some interesting facts were indeed unearthed.

This manor house was built for Thomas and Mary Lakeman, a wealthy merchant and brewery family, and legend has it that the other three properties were constructed for their daughters as a wedding gift.

Several years later, the Rev H. F. Lyte, the author of that immortal hymn "Abide with Me", resided here temporarily before taking up permanent residence at Berry Head House.

It was, however, the next family, William and Maria Pellow Green and their seven children, who for reasons best known to themselves made their lasting impression on Burton Villa. Whether it was due to grief, unhappiness, illness or some other major trauma that affected their lives during this period we will never know, yet over one hundred and fifty years later this family were reluctant, in spirit, to vacate what had been their home for so many years.

When new owners with their two children moved in, in March 1970, they were faced with a major task; the house had been sorely neglected and had fallen into disrepair to the extent that only one downstairs room was habitable, as the wiring was condemned and candles were the only form of lighting.

One evening, shortly afterwards, when the children were fast asleep, Shirley and her husband wanted to take a look at the upstairs of the house. Before leaving the room they noticed that their two-year-old son had kicked off his bedclothes but, as it was a warm evening, they left him as he was. On returning some twenty minutes later, they were amazed to find that the child had been neatly tucked in! This was to be the first of many strange incidents.

In the first year, during certain times of the early evening, one was able to detect the strong smell of pipe tobacco wafting through the main downstairs hall. This was surprising in itself, for no-one in the household smoked …

During the restoration work on one of the top rooms, which seemed to have been used as a nursery or playroom a long, long time ago, the names of three children were discovered, written on the wall directly beneath the window. As little importance was attached to this find at that time, the names were covered over.

With the work now completed, the family moved upstairs, and Shirley recalled how she started to be awakened at night by the sound of children's voices floating across the room. This was then followed by the appearance in the doorway of the figure of a lady which she described as "wearing a long white cotton nightdress with sleeves, her shoulder-length hair tied back and carrying a brass candlestick; in fact she gave the distinct impression of being an olden-day nanny."

This mysterious lady was also to offer more materialistic evidence to her authenticity for, on several occasions, children's well-manicured fingernail clippings were discovered on an upstairs table.

On other nights when Shirley awoke she would experience an ice-cold sensation and an extremely "chilly" atmosphere prevailing in the room for no obvious reason. It was during these times that she observed a restful blue glow suspended directly above her which seemed to contain some sort of mystic energy for, try as she might, she was unable to sit up – as if this incomprehensible force was controlling her every move.

Even friends who have stayed at Burton Villa over the years have experienced the sound of the laughter and voices of the "never seen" children, accompanied by the "lady in white" who is presumably watching over them.

It should be emphasised that Shirley's husband was a total non-believer in anything appertaining to the supernatural, yet he admits that when his wife was away for three weeks one year, he awoke and distinctly heard the sound of children's laughter, and he watched as the bedclothes were slowly pulled off him during the night. He was completely alone in the house.

These facts only show that an "influence" or "apparition" residing in a premises can convert even a person who has a negative attitude to the unknown.

Knock, Knock ... Who's There? – Elkins Hill

The view over Torbay from Elkins Hill is truly panoramic so, after spending many holidays at Brixham, Marie and her husband John finally located the house of their choice in this area and took up residence in July 1974. Although neighbours and friends had already declared the property to be haunted, not too much importance was attached to this; the couple settled in at their new peaceful abode ... and were soon to find out that the stories had been true!

The first incidents were explained away as pure coincidence, for the Christian names of the previous owners had also been Marie and John. Then when they moved in, they were placing one of their most treasured possessions on the mantelpiece – an antique clock in black marble – when they discovered that the previous occupants also had an identical clock, which had stood in the same place for years.

Shortly afterwards they began to experience a musty smell, lingering about in certain parts of the house; they found that they were able to walk in and out of this. It was not

unlike the presence of an elderly person, and during these encounters they had the distinct impression that they were being watched.

Incidents seemed to become activated when visitors came to stay. Marie recalls that on the day of the royal wedding between Prince Charles and Lady Diana Spencer, she was alone in the house when she heard a group of people, presumably her friends, enter and walk along the hall. But when she went to look, no one was there …

Then, only two days later, the family who were staying with her were again thought to be heard to enter through the front door and ascend the stairs – at which point John decided to see if they would like a pot of tea. For some strange reason Marie told her husband that it was only their eerie "invisible" visitors. Undeterred, John searched all the rooms and, to his utter astonishment, found them all to be empty – yet he was aware that the hair on his neck was standing proud and the atmosphere had become unnaturally cold.

Marie and John have even heard someone come out of the front bedroom, descend the stairs and go back up again, followed by the sound of music … yet upon investigation, have found the house to be completely empty. There was also the time they heard a group of people on the balcony outside … but nobody was visible.

It is now no surprise when household items disappear and are sometimes discovered in places that have been previously searched. One evening in the 1980s, whilst in the lounge, they were subjected to the most intensely loud knocking sound on the wall, close to where John was sitting. This was followed by a regular evening vigil, when the front and back doors would be knocked simultaneously. However, whatever strange "ghost" was performing these actions, it never physically showed itself, for this prankster spirit was nowhere to be seen – although Marie has felt that she has at times bumped into some invisible form, which has sent shivers up and down her spine. The inexplicable hauntings have continued …!

The Haunted Cottage – Overgang

When William of Orange landed at Brixham, with five hundred ships and twenty thousand foot soldiers on 5 November 1688, his troops were to be encamped on Furzeham Common. In order to reach their destination, it was necessary for them to march up the hill directly from the quay. The soldiers referred to this route as the "Way up" or "Way over"; in their native Dutch the direct translation was "Overgang", and that is the name still given to this hill.

Before 1700, six cottages were constructed at the foot of this hill on a site we now know as Custom Court. At least one of them has experienced its fair share of paranormal occurrences over this time span.

Early in 1949, Farthing Cottage was up for sale. When Mrs Hill, who was an accomplished artist, saw it advertised in the estate agent's window, she experienced an uncontrollable desire to own this property.

However, when you have only the meagre sum of 4s 6d ($22\frac{1}{2}$p) in your bank account and the cottage of your dreams is £1,500, nothing short of a miracle will do … and that is what happened! Whether you call it fate or destiny, the local bank looked on the transaction favourably and thus helped Mrs Hill to purchase the cottage.

Mrs Hill's mother, Mrs Elizabeth Jane Rice, who was living in Wolverhampton, would spend her holidays with her daughter at the cottage, but all was not well, for she repeatedly exclaimed that she felt some undesirable "force" or "power" was prevalent in the surroundings. At the time her daughter, who, I must add, felt nothing but an immense feeling of happiness about the place, dismissed her mother's comments as imagination.

In 1950, due to personal circumstances, Mrs Rice gave up her home in the Midlands and reluctantly moved in with her daughter at Farthing Cottage, still convinced that there was a prevailing ghostly atmosphere.

During this time the ghostly happenings increased, for the lady would constantly remark about the people she saw walking about her room at night, and in particular described a man who repeatedly came up and down the stairs.

Although by now Mrs Rice had developed an intense fear of the supernatural, this ghost did display a kind nature on one occasion. The elderly lady recalled how one night, when she was descending the narrow, dimly-lit staircase, she missed her footing and began to fall forward. As she reached out in an attempt to save herself, the mysterious gentleman grasped both her arms firmly, steadied her from falling, and averted what might have been a tragic accident.

The hauntings became so intense that Mrs Hill was disturbed one dark, windy evening by noises coming from her mother's bedroom. Upon investigation she found the window wide open, the curtains blowing full length into the room and her mother brandishing a tennis racquet, trying, in vain, to "get the demons out" as she explained.

The dark shrouded figure of a man was also once observed trying to remove certain floorboards in the sitting room on the first floor. Is it possible that he might be the "ghost" of one of the many sea captains or mariners who must surely have dwelt in that cottage over a period of nearly three hundred years? Was he looking for something precious that he had hidden? And could that mystery still be beneath the floorboards?

As the situation had become so intolerable, both Mrs Hill and her mother moved out to alternative accommodation in King Street. Farthing Cottage was then rented out, which would seem, to all intents and purposes, the end of the story ... Yet further information was still to be forthcoming.

For obvious reasons, no mention was made to the new tenants about previous "spirits" or encounters at this quaint and picturesque cottage, so after some time had elapsed Mrs Hill paid a courtesy call on these people to see if everything was satisfactory. She was informed by the lady of the house that since they had moved in many of their friends had visited them and some of these had expressed comments on how they felt a distinct "presence" in certain areas of the cottage.

One group which stayed with her brought along a clairvoyant friend who, after only two days, announced to all present that Farthing Cottage was haunted by a man called "Johnnie" who was emitting a particularly happy feeling as he travelled through the rooms, and that he had been returning to the cottage for many years. Perhaps Johnnie, whoever he might be, is still returning to the cottage to this day?

Once a Year and the "Prankster" – Fore Street

In these days of high-speed trains, supersonic flights and cross-channel ferries, it is almost impossible to comprehend that at one time the only mode of transportation was by coach and horses.

At that time Fore Street in Brixham would echo with the sound of hooves on the cobbled thoroughfare as travellers composed themselves for the arduous journey ahead to London. No doubt if the thick stone walls of the Globe, which was built in 1780, could divulge their secrets, they would offer up many a tale of not only happy events but also incidents relating to the anguish, torment, heartache and uncertainty of those bygone days – it is these experiences, more than any other, that seem to leave their traumatic presence on a property.

In January 1971, which was only eight months after Ken and his wife took over the tenancy at the Globe Inn, HMS *Palister* paid her regular yearly visit to Brixham and, as on previous occasions, the crew stayed at the inn for one or two nights. After their departure it was noticed that the customary "visitors' book", which was always kept upstairs, had gone missing. It was assumed, quite naturally, that one of the crew members had walked away with it as a joke.

The following January, Ken was sitting behind the bar when he chanced to look down and there, covered in dust and lying in full view, was the visitors' book! The very next day, HMS *Palister* steamed into Brixham. So what form of prankster had gone to the trouble to hide the book for exactly a year?

No further incidents of this nature occurred for nearly twelve months, until Ken's mother, who was unwell at the time, decided to make the journey down from Sheffield to stay with them at the Globe.

In order to listen out for his mother during the night, Ken propped open both bedroom doors, his own being held ajar by a metal waste paper bin. At around one o'clock in the morning, the bin was knocked over – which awakened both Ken and his wife. As they sat up in bed, they distinctly heard the unmistakable sound of hobnail boots walking on bare floorboards around their bed, even though the bedroom was fully carpeted at the time!

When their two daughters stayed, this mysterious "phenomenon" decided to stage another exhibition of its power, by continuously moving a curtain covering a wardrobe area to and fro, all night long. The girls vowed that they would never stay in that room again!

During 1986 Ken was taken seriously ill and to aid his recuperation he was transferred to a convalescent home at Newton Abbot. There he met a lady in her mid-eighties who declared that she had been born at the Globe Inn, Brixham, as her mother had been a servant there all those years ago. The old lady enquired eagerly whether the ghost of the elderly gentleman dressed in tweeds was still wandering up and down the stairs at the inn?

The next tenants, David and Wendy Kennedy, moved into the Globe in the early 1990s, and within a very short time the well-wishing locals were regaling them with stories and events of a ghostly nature appertaining to their new environment. However, never having had any previous encounters of this type in their lives before, the Kennedys did not treat these tales too seriously.

After only three months, Wendy started finding things were becoming mysteriously mislaid, or going missing for a time. On the first occasion a piece of embroidery, belonging to an aunt, which was packed away safely in a box exactly one year ago, materialised itself on the lounge floor, the very day before the aunt was due to visit!

All evidence seems to suggest that this prankster ghost is of the female gender, for it chooses only ladies' apparel, such as underclothes, jewellery or dressing gowns, which always go missing at night, only to reappear several days later in places where they will be obviously discovered during the day.

A recent incident of a more disturbing nature took place late one night. Wendy was sitting up in bed reading when she suddenly became aware of the curious sound of what she described as shallow breathing coming from another part of the bedroom. After listening to it for some time, she then decided to wake her husband – however, before he had time to sit up, the breathing stopped.

I had the opportunity of examining and photographing the three bedrooms in which these happenings have taken place. In one particular room I experienced a distinct drop in temperature which was in direct contrast to the bright sunny day on which I visited.

Over the last thirty years, whenever new people have moved in, or when major building, restoration or electrical work is carried out, this mischievous "power" seems to become recharged, as if confirming to those present the very fact of its authenticity.

One thing is certain, anyone who has the audacity to scoff at the ghost's abilities is soon subjected to a demonstration – as an unsuspecting fisherman found out when a towel propelled itself across the room and into his face! A local in the front bar announced that "there is no such thing as ghosts" ; over the next few days he witnessed his pint of beer topple over on the bar without being touched, and a glass slide off a shelf onto the floor of its own accord … he then changed his opinion!

Don't Call Us, We'll Call You – Temperance Steps

When John and Sue rented a cottage on Temperance Steps, they noticed that a telephone had been installed by some previous tenant, but it had now been disconnected from the exchange.

They both decided that as the instrument was not working, and as they had no need to make any calls, no purpose could be served by paying out to have it reconnected, and that was how the situation was left.

At around two o'clock one morning, some ten months later, John was awakened by the sound of a ringing telephone. Knowing that it could not possibly be in the cottage, he turned over in an endeavour to get back to sleep.

The persistent ringing continued so, mystified by this inexplicable incident, he made his way slowly down the stairs and warily lifted the receiver.

The voice at the other end was that of his sister Bernadette, who was regrettably the bearer of sad news; John's father had passed away and she was naturally anxious to convey the unhappy tidings to her brother.

John asked her how she had obtained a number for him to a property where no telephone was registered? Quite surprised, she explained that she had contacted directory enquiries who had helped her without any hesitation.

Still somewhat sceptical about this strange "happening", John went out next day and rang directory enquiries himself, only to be told that there was no possible way that they could have given out a number to an address where, according to their records, no telephone existed.

Unsatisfied with their explanation, he related to them the incident which had taken place in the early hours of the morning, and even told them the number his sister had been given.

Closer investigation disclosed that there was no logical way that this number could connect with the cottage, for it had been allocated to another subscriber. Still unconvinced, John asked Sue to stand by the phone whilst he went to a call box and dialled the number.

After several moments the phone was answered, yet it was not Sue's voice on the other end, but that of the Strand Bakery! John replaced the receiver, still none the wiser, and was no nearer solving the mystery. That telephone never rang in the cottage again.

The Ghosts of Brixham

A Stitch in Time – Middle Street

After my first programme with BBC Radio Devon, on the Chris Langmore *Late Night Show*, I received numerous letters, phone calls and even notes pushed through my front door, on strange happenings in the community.

As a matter of procedure, I always interviewed the people concerned in order to verify the authenticity of their story. Sometimes, on visits to two entirely separate locations, different fragments of the same story are divulged, which then enables me to piece together the complete episode. This was the case when I visited Nick, a tailor in Middle Street.

During the 1980s, a lady friend of his, named Tina, came down from London to spend her two-week holiday with him. At that time the upstairs attic was used as a bedroom, as the floor below was devoted to a workshop area.

On that particular night the bedroom door had been left ajar for ventilation. At about 3 a.m. Nick was awakened by Tina, who was sitting bolt upright in bed, clearly rather perplexed about something. She stated emphatically that she had just seen a ghost. In order to put her mind at rest, Nick conducted a search of the entire property from top to bottom, yet he was unable to find one single shred of evidence to substantiate this "sighting".

At breakfast the next morning, the previous night's incident was discussed in greater detail. Tina explained that for some unknown reason she had woken up abruptly and been compelled to gaze in the direction of the open door.

There, looking into the bedroom, had been a little, grey-haired old lady dressed completely in black, with a black shawl wrapped around her shoulders. At the point when Tina turned round to wake Nick, the old lady disappeared.

Some twelve months later, a customer who lived locally in Pring's Court brought in some dressmaking alterations. In the course of conversation, she happened to mention that many years ago these premises had been occupied by another tailor and his wife, whom she remembered distinctly because the man was very tall, whereas his wife was a sweet little grey-haired old lady who always dressed in black and never went anywhere without her black shawl wrapped around her shoulders!

For all intents and purposes I was quite prepared at that stage to consider this story complete. Yet the very next day I was to discover more about this mysterious sighting from an entirely different source.

I was in the Long Bar public house, off Fore Street, talking to the landlord Roy Perrett about his ancestors (who were amongst some of the first settlers in Brixham) when Roy happened to mention his grandparents.

His grandfather, who had died in 1950, had been a ladies' bespoke tailor who worked in the attic of the house where he lived in Middle Street. The coincidence here is that this house was the very one where my story had started the day before.

Roy described how, after his grandfather's death, his grandmother Anna Marie, who was a lovely, little, grey-haired old lady, dressed in black with a shawl around her shoulders, pined away at the loss of her partner, to the extent that some six years later she also died.

The doctor was unable to trace any physical failure or illness which could have caused the demise of Grandma Anna Marie, yet it would seem that he did find the reason – for on the certificate the cause of death was clearly shown: the old lady had died of a "Broken Heart".

Poetic Justice – Bolton Street

In 1988, whilst in a retail shop in Bolton Street, an elderly lady related a series of puzzling events which she had been involved in over a period of time.

As she explained, it all started one night just as she was about to retire to bed. For some unknown reason her subconscious instructed her to leave pen and paper on the bedside cabinet.

Sometime during the night, the lady arose from her bed and sat down in front of the blank paper. It must be stressed at this point that at no time did she awake. The only recollection she had of this experience was "as if I was in a very distant far off dream", she stated.

On awaking, her first impulse was to glance over at the bedside cabinet and there, written in beautiful, long flowing script was a well-composed poem. This strange phenomenon took place regularly after that, so much so that she found that if the room was filled with a strange fragrance, similar to that of spring flowers, when she awoke, another poem had been compiled. Whenever this "force" was present it must have emitted this long-lasting aroma, whilst transcribing these verses to paper.

Now armed with enough material to compile a book, the lady sent off the entire collection of poems to a publisher. She was subsequently informed that the entire "works" had been written in the hand and style of a famous poet of a bygone era! For reasons best known to himself, he had deemed it necessary to continue his talents through this unsuspecting lady.

The Show Must Go On – Bolton Cross

Superstitions are commonplace in the theatrical profession, where one never opens a telegram until after a performance, or you wish a fellow Thespian "good luck" by telling them to "break a leg". Yet these often strange and deep-rooted beliefs are part of our everyday culture and are not therefore considered bizarre in any way.

The late John Slater will probably be best remembered for his portrayal of Sergeant Stone in the long-running television series Z Cars. The cockney actor was an extremely superstitious character, to the extent that off screen he would never turn away a wandering gypsy from his home before crossing their palm with silver, as he was convinced that they had deep-rooted ancestral powers.

In 1972 the Brixham theatre staged a comedy thriller entitled *Wanted One Body* in which John wore a costume comprising of pin-striped trousers, grey gaiters and black boots.

The following year he undertook an exhausting and demanding role in the production of *Reluctant Heroes*, but for one who already had a serious heart condition, it was too

much and sadly, during the Christmas of 1973, he died. As a tribute to his memory, his wife Betty arranged for a bust of her husband to be placed in the Brixham theatre as a form of remembrance.

It was then that strange incidents started to happen. That very evening, when the manageress was preparing the bar in readiness for the night's performance, she caught sight of a figure walking down the passageway towards the artistes' resting rooms. Knowing them to be locked, she immediately went to investigate ... and found no-one.

Later that night, the lady who ran the box office was in the same corridor, bending down to pick up her bag, when she saw the figure of a man approaching, so she moved her basket in order to give him room to pass. However, when she straightened up and looked to see who it was ... the corridor was empty!

Both ladies related the incidents to each other on the following day, and at that time neither was able to offer any plausible explanation, yet on one detail they were both agreed – whoever it was they saw, he was wearing pin-striped trousers, grey gaiters and black boots!

From then on many strange things started to happen: stage lights would suddenly come on, for no apparent reason, when the theatre was empty; orchestra cue lights would be found on in the morning, when everything had been methodically turned off the night before. The back-stage stairs became so "eerie" that staff refused to venture near this area, as they were convinced that some presence was continually walking behind them.

In 1987 a strong, almost uncanny, "influence" was experienced during a summer season show. On one particular evening, an electrician had set up the sound mixer unit and lighting board ready for the next day's performance. But upon his arrival next morning, he was intrigued to find that the equipment had been altered overnight and the lighting sequence changed to resemble how it had been operated in the early 1970s!

It became generally accepted, by the staff at the theatre, that the mysterious happenings could well be the antics of the "ghost" of John Slater, for after all he was a devoted artiste and who knows, perhaps he was reluctant to leave the theatre that he loved so much, and therefore still resides there to this very day?

Heart-Broken – Milton Street

Many stories have been related about the "haunted" Black House on Milton Street, where so many mysterious happenings have been experienced over the years. Records have established that there was a dwelling on this site as far back as the 1100s, which was then associated with St Mary's Church and used by novice clergy whilst undertaking their ecclesiastical studies.

Located directly over the top front window are the dates 1457 – 1913. It was during this period that this was the home of the well-to-do Gillard family, who became landowners, squires, merchants and solicitors; in fact at one time their wealth consisted in their owning no less than 20 per cent of all Brixham.

However, it was not until the 1600s that an incident took place that has resulted in the Black House being haunted ever since. At that time Squire Gillard had an elder son who was not only expected to carry on the family name, but also to conduct himself in a proper and professional manner. Yet, as we all know, the path of life never runs smoothly and young Master Gillard met and fell in love with a dairymaid, well beneath his status, whose family lived and worked on the estate.

Unknown to the young man, his father found out and immediately adopted a plan of action. Firstly, he sent his son away to sea on the pretext that he was to learn the fundamentals of buying and selling merchandise in different parts of the world, and secondly, again without his son's knowledge, he paid off the girl's family on the understanding that she would never have anything to do with his son again.

Some considerable time later, Master Gillard returned from his voyage to his home port of Brixham and was making his way on horseback towards home when he passed St Mary's Church and noticed that a wedding was taking place. He stopped to admire the bride when, to his total anguish, he observed that it was his beloved dairymaid on the arm of another man.

Heart-broken, he spurred his horse up to the Black House, removed the reins, and in sheer desolation hanged himself from the big tree outside the house.

From that very day on, the tragedy has left its "ghosts" for, during the hours of darkness, the clatter of young Master Gillard's phantom horse can be heard on cobbles at the rear of the property as it returns home riderless. The presence of the remorseful Squire is also experienced as he wanders aimlessly through the house seeking to atone for his unforgivable action!

The Haunted Chapel – Elkins Hill

In the days before radar and other navigational instruments, returning trawlermen would set their sights on the tall spire of the church away up on Elkins Hill as a guide into Brixham harbour.

In 1850 this had been an area of common land, so the wealthy, God-fearing Elkins family constructed their own private chapel, complete with beautiful stained-glass windows, on this site where they would worship together in seclusion.

For reasons best known to themselves, the ground was never consecrated, nor was this chapel assigned to any specific denomination. It did, however, contain a makeshift altar, but lacked any seating arrangements.

Some years later the Elkins family emigrated to Australia and were never heard of again. Subsequently this lovely little chapel became derelict for quite some time. It was not used again until the closure of a school in New Road necessitated the transfer of the pupils to alternative accommodation, and the committee decided on the now empty Elkins chapel.

As the pupils were all children of fisherfolk they were mainly given seafaring instruction rather than normal scholastic education, for it is to be appreciated that in those days reading and writing was considered far less important than gaining a knowledgeable experience of the sea, as these children would be required to commence work at a very early age.

Whilst children elsewhere were taught to recite the Lord's Prayer, the pupils at this chapel had an entirely different quotation drummed into them, which went as follows: *Green to Green, Red to Red, Perfect Safety Straight Ahead. If upon the Starboard Red Appear, It's your Duty to keep Clear. When in Danger or in Doubt, Always keep a Sharp Lookout.* This was considered the rule of the sea and had to be memorised by each and every pupil.

When the Board school was built in 1890, all the pupils were transferred to these larger premises, which are still in existence in Furzeham to this very day.

Being abandoned, the chapel fell into a state of disrepair until an extremely religious old fisherman nicknamed "Fishcombe Jerry" decided that this was a heaven-sent gift where he could house his pigs and chickens for free.

He became so possessive and fanatical about his newly acquired property that he refused to allow any intruders over the threshold and guarded the place with his very life.

After twelve years, Jerry claimed squatter's rights and legally obtained the old chapel. Whether this was the beginning of his misfortune we will never know, but from then on things went from bad to worse and within two years he died.

Shortly afterwards the premises were turned into a workshop by a carpenter who carried out all the work for the local undertaker.

One time a carpenter and a young boy apprentice were working late into the night in an effort to complete a pair of coffins for the next day. When it had become dark outside, the lad started to experience the feeling of a decidedly chilly atmosphere surrounding him, which became steadily more predominant as the night wore on. Finally, gripped with an uncontrollable fear, he downed tools and fled.

Somewhat mystified by what he considered had been an overactive imagination on the part of the apprentice, the carpenter returned to his work. That was until he too found himself repeatedly glancing over his shoulder and felt the "presence" of something weird and unnatural in the workshop.

The Ghosts of Brixham

When he heard the strains of the hymn "Rock of Ages" being sung faintly behind him, he became petrified, unable to move for quite some time. When he finally plucked up enough courage to turn around, there in the frame of the east window was the unmistakable form of Fishcombe Jerry holding a lantern and staring down at him.

It was exactly twelve months to the very day that Jerry had passed away!

In 1950 the chapel and spire were razed to the ground and flats were built in their place. However, in one of the rear flats which had been constructed directly over the original east window, no electrical appliance would function after dark for a full 365 days.

Money Isn't Everything – Pring's Court

The Pomeroy family lived at Berry Pomeroy Castle, Totnes, between 1066 and 1547 and St Margaret's Tower is reputed to be haunted to this very day. However, that is another story and can be found in Deryck Seymour's book *The Ghosts of Berry Pomeroy Castle*. I only mentioned this to illustrate how far back the origins of this well-known family name can be traced.

No 2, Pring's Court, as we know it today, is a lovely Georgian cottage which was designed by an architect named Churchill and built in 1779. It became the home of John and Margaret who used it primarily as a bed-and-breakfast house, yet the relaxing holidaymakers who have had the pleasure of staying there are possibly oblivious to the history which surrounds this dwelling.

In the early 1800s, the adjacent cottages in this Court were dens for smugglers where they stored their contraband of French brandy, gin and such like away from the prying eyes of the ever watchful Duty men.

However this cottage was destined to be a far more respectable establishment, for in the early part of 1810, John Hine, Henry Joseph Holdsworth and Roger Pomeroy founded the Brixham Bank at these premises.

All went well for just over thirteen years, but then both Hine and Holdsworth died within a short period of each other, leaving Roger Pomeroy as the sole proprietor. Disaster was almost inevitable: due to lack of business sense, the bank collapsed on 19 March 1824 and subsequently Roger Pomeroy was made bankrupt. This must have been a traumatic experience, not to mention casting a slur on the ancestral name.

In 1830 a new banking partnership was formed under the name of Brooking & Browse, which in 1837 became Browse & Co, only to change in 1839 to Green & Co.

The memory of the Brixham Bank has now long since faded; so too has the presence of Roger Pomeroy ... Or has it?

In the comfortable lounge of this cottage a "presence" still remained which I personally experienced during a visit. Between 12 noon and 12.30 p.m. each day the temperature dropped considerably and the room became unnaturally cold, no matter how much the heating was increased. It only lasted for this short period, yet it persisted all the time that John and Margaret were in residence.

And on the first-floor landing, which is the same floor where the strongroom was kept during the banking days, one encounters a pleasant but mysterious aroma from time to time. It was described to me as unlike any household cosmetic smell, but resembling something sweet and pungent which one would liken to freshly cut flowers in the early morning.

"Lost Forever" – Berry Head

When I first met Mr William J. Davis I was pleased to learn that we shared the same inquisitive mutual interest into the realms of mysterious experiences. This gentleman, who had travelled around the world several times and visited over a hundred different countries in his lifetime, had many unusual and inexplicable incidents to relate.

Yet for all his globe-trotting stories, one of the most sinister and fascinating episodes he had uncovered had taken place right here, in his own home town, over the last two centuries.

A favourite venue for all visitors to Brixham is Berry Head, where the scenic cliffs rise majestically over two hundred feet out of the sea. The whole area is saturated in historical happenings as far back as Roman times, when the first encampment was constructed.

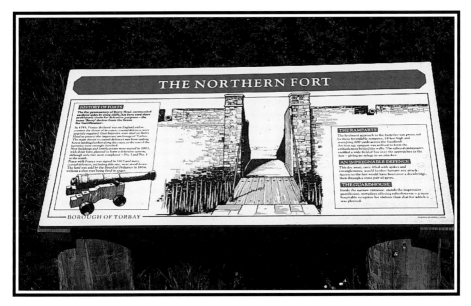

When France declared war on England, there appeared to be a threat of invasion by the General Napoleon, so two forts were built on Berry Head to protect the area from possible attack.

It was in 1803, when an existing storehouse on the site was being demolished in preparation for these fortifications, that the skeleton of a young man was uncovered. The news of this discovery spread throughout the area and legend has it that someone wanted the head for comparison on archaeological work that was being carried out. The remainder of the skeleton was buried in the Berry Head cemetery, which was at the time a makeshift resting place adjoining the Military Hospital.

Within twenty years these premises had become Berry Head House and subsequently became the home of the Rev. H. F. Lyte, the author of that well-loved hymn "Abide With Me".

It was whilst levelling a mound of earth in the garden that the Reverend unearthed a quantity of human bones, which also included the remains of the young man. These were covered up immediately and a small monument was erected bearing a somewhat mysterious inscription "To the Unknown Dead".

Several years passed before a series of inexplicable sounds were heard from the vicinity of the monument. At first people paid little attention, as they were convinced that these were the mating calls of a pigeon that could be heard in the still night air.

On some nights the sound was more penetrating than others and seemed to take on a distinct similarity to a human voice. As the calling persisted, greater interest was taken and, by many, the theory of the pigeon began to be replaced by a more bizarre explanation, for there were days when the sound continued incessantly and became so noticeably clearer that it was likened to the sound of a lost soul calling … "I want my head … I want my head … I want my head …"

Not many years ago, a guest staying at what was by then the Berry Head Hotel was so annoyed by the nightly disturbance of what he assumed to be a persistent pigeon that he offered £50 to anyone who could locate the noisy bird. To this day nobody has ever laid claim to this reward …

It's Your Move – Berry Head

One of the most bizarre incidents I ever encountered was concerning a lady called Edna, who had been subjected to a traumatic "poltergeist" experience; to this very day, I still find it difficult to comprehend how she resisted this evil force for so long.

It all started back in September 1974, when she was living in Exeter and undertook a council house exchange with a property in Brixham. This she was delighted with, for it was on a picturesque site close to the Berry Head area. On first reflections she thought it unusual that bolts had been fitted to the *outside* of each door; however, not attaching too much importance to this matter, the unsightly objects were quickly removed.

For the next two months everything went well and her younger son settled into his new school. She then became surprised to learn that her elder son was feeling uncomfortable in the property, had given up his job and was returning to Exeter.

On the very first night that Edna and her younger son were alone in the house together, while playing cards, they became aware of an inexplicable metallic knocking sound coming from the front window. But when they drew back the curtains to investigate … no-one was there!

Two days later, whilst in the kitchen, Edna heard the distinct sound of heavy footsteps in the bedroom above, followed by the repetitive sound of knocking. Their dog had positioned himself at the foot of the stairs and was growling ferociously. When her son returned home from the shops he asked what the noise was upstairs, to which Edna could offer no answer. So jokingly he shouted up, "If you want a cup of tea, knock once for yes or twice for no!" … Whatever macabre entity was listening that afternoon, it knocked twice loudly and then stopped. The metallic knocking sound on the window, which I might add was loud enough to drown the television programmes, commenced regularly each evening as soon as the lounge curtains were drawn and would continue relentlessly until one o'clock each morning.

Then the pattern of strange "hauntings" began to change. Just before Christmas, they were trying to watch television when the monotonous knocking stopped abruptly and the standard lamp started moving on its own, as if charged with some mysterious energy. It threw off its shade onto the floor and, to their sheer horror, travelled about the room in all directions!

On Christmas Eve Edna's mother, together with relatives, arrived at about 8.30 p.m. and, just thirty minutes later, the standard lamp was giving a "command performance" for its new and larger audience. It now adopted an aggressive attitude by propelling itself around, falling over, righting itself, breaking the coffee table and finally destroying the Christmas decorations.

The antics continued on Christmas Day, when the lamp narrowly missed Edna's young son but she was not so fortunate, for she received a resounding blow on the arm. In sheer desperation they transferred the lamp to the garage.

This poltergeist which had possessed their home seemed able to manifest itself in many different forms, for they started hearing strange noises from all over the house, their names being called when no-one else was around and a series of coloured lights emerging from the carpet and then vaporising into smoke right in front of them, whilst throughout the house all the doors would open and close of their own accord.

Some days seemed more active, for they began observing a black shadowy "apparition" descending the stairs and disappearing through the front wall; the entire contents of the bedroom dressing table being strewn around the room; and a constant bombardment of electric light bulbs springing out of their sockets.

The nights had taken on a different type of torment, for now they were being subjected to a spate of uncanny knocking sounds, this time from between the floorboards upstairs. This strange phenomenon would commence at precisely eleven o'clock each night and continue until four o'clock the next morning. Should they attempt to complain in any way, then their beds would be lifted momentarily off the floor.

Edna made two desperate attempts at reprisal, firstly by hanging a crucifix on the wall of her mother's bedroom, and secondly by summoning the local priest in an effort to rid the premises of "evil spirits". Disappointingly, neither of these efforts made the slightest difference.

It was to be three painful years of "hell" before Edna and her son admitted defeat and finally moved out of the area. It is not known whether that house is still possessed to this day, but one thing is certain – in the four years after Edna moved away, no less than three different families came and went without reason …

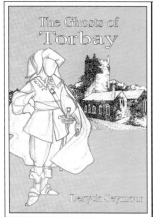

If you have enjoyed this book, the chances are that you will enjoy the other titles in the same series!

The Ghosts of Berry Pomeroy Castle is a collection of psychic experiences which people have had at or near the castle. Visit it and read the book – you might be surprised to find that the strange sounds, feelings or atmosphere are not just in your imagination – other people have felt and seen them too!

The Ghosts of Torbay chronicles the spooky, mysterious, strange and inexplicable ghostly goings-on in the whole of Torbay, from Torquay to Brixham. It tells of the experiences of authors Beverly Nichols and Rudyard Kipling, and of hauntings in places as diverse as churches and pubs.

A town as ancient and packed with history as Totnes must surely have a surfeit of spirits. And indeed *The Ghosts of Totnes* are gathered together in this book: a host of ghosts, a selection of spirits or a fact file of phantoms – you will have to make up your own mind whether or not they really exist!

We all know Plymouth is steeped in history – Sir Francis Drake, the Pilgrim Fathers, the Civil War siege, the Plymouth Blitz – but did you know it is also steeped in ghosts? It has haunted houses, spectral soldiers and sailors, and phantom-infested pubs! Nancy Hammonds has collected spooky stories and reports of weird phenomena and put together this entertaining collection of true ghost stories as told by local people who have encountered the supernatural. If you like ghostly tales, then you will certainly enjoy *The Ghosts of Plymouth*!

And in *The Ghosts of Exeter* you can read of ghostly monks and nuns, highwaymen and sailors, cats and dogs, devils and sprites. No wonder Exeter's reputation as a "haunted city" is growing fast!